Another Dirty

30

More Words Smart People Misuse

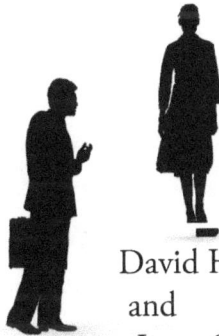

David Hatcher
and
Lane Goddard

LANDABOOKS

Published in the United States of America by LandaBooks.

ISBN 978-0-9729920-1-5

LANDABOOKS

1873 Meadowbrook Drive
Winston-Salem, NC 27104
336.354.8238
480.247.5750 Fax
info@landabooks.com
www.landabooks.com

Cover design by
One Hero Creative
Winston-Salem, NC

Contents

Introduction

If you read our original *Dirty Thirty* book, we hope you learned how to distinguish between similar words and—like other readers who contacted us—found the exercises and memory hooks useful.

Some readers suggested additional words they had trouble with and would like to see included in a follow-on. *Another Dirty Thirty* is the result of that feedback. We think that you'll enjoy it and that it will help you choose the right word with confidence.

You'll find an explanation after each set of words (usually a pair, sometimes trios or even quartets). After the explanation, you'll have a short exercise to make sure you understand and to help lock the meanings in your memory. (You'll be able to check your knowledge immediately, because answers are upside-down at the bottom of each exercise.)

After every six exercises, you'll have a pair of cumulative exercises including all the words covered in those six. So in all, you'll have forty exercises—one on each specific group of confusable words, as well as ten cumulative exercises.

We hope that you enjoy learning about these words, that you have fun using them, and that they help you in your speaking and writing.

Aid-Aide

To *aid* (verb) is to help out or assist, and *aid* (noun) is the help given: "They hurried in to aid the flood victims, who deeply appreciated the aid provided."

An *aide* is a helper, an assistant. The term is most-often applied to a junior officer whose duty is to accompany and assist a senior officer: "The general's aide made sure that everything was in order." But it can be applied to anyone whose role is to assist (to aid) someone else.

NOTE: Although it's not as likely to cause confusion, it's worth noting here that *AIDS* is the name given to a serious and widespread health problem (Acquired Immune Deficiency Syndrome).

Our aide has prepared a little exercise to aid your retention.

Exercise: Aid-Aide

In each numbered item, circle or underline your choice.

1. The nurse's aid/aide came to the aid/aide of the overworked EMT.

2. The aid/aide she provided may have aided the recovery of the injured fire chief's aid/aide.

3. The student who was given the job of instructor's aid/aide was supposed to provide aid/aide to struggling freshmen.

4. The braided cord on his shoulder identified him as the personal aid/aide to the commander (his aid/aide de camp).

5. When the doctor and his aid/aide arrived, they were welcomed by the maid, who provided aid/aide to the admiral's aid/aide.

6. The aid's/aide's grateful family offered to pay the maid for her aid/aide to the aid/aide. (*Optional bonus:* But she graciously demured/demurred.)

7. The braid displayed by the aid/aide was an aid/aide to identifying him.

8. During the briefing, the aid/aide displayed the map of the area, which was a valuable aid/aide to understanding the situation.

9. After the parade, the aid/aide was dismayed by the lack of aid/aide provided by the physician's aid/aide.

10. The professor's aid/aide gave the students this spelling aid/aide: "The word for an assisting person ends with an *e*, like *he* and *she*. So if you're talking about a he or she, end the word with an *e* (aide). But if you're talking about help, *don't do* it—instead, end with a *d* (aid)."

10. aide, aid.
6. aide's, aid, aide (demurred); 7. aide, aid; 8. aide, aid; 9. aide, aid, aide;
1. aide, aid; 2. aid, aide; 3. aide, aid; 4. aide, aide; 5. aide, aid, aide;

7

Allude-Refer

We're in a slightly awkward position here, because our own opinion about these words doesn't precisely line up with the opinions of many other advisors. To be fair, let's start with the opinion of those others.

They say that *allude* should be used only to mean an indirect reference, as when a speaker doesn't choose to specifically name whatever's referred to. For example, if Joe says "I know your husband has had some difficulty with the authorities…," he's alluding to those difficulties. But if he says "I know your husband has been arrested three times on bad-check charges…," he's referring to them.

We could list at least a half-dozen respected references that tell us to use *allude* in that way only. So why do we demur? Why don't we go along with those authorities? Well, we do, sort of. That is, we advise (or at least suggest) that you follow that practice, but only because your readers and listeners may well have been taught that it's wrong to do otherwise, and may think ill of you if you don't.

The reason we don't support it whole-heartedly is simple—lots of intelligent and highly competent writers and speakers choose to ignore the rule. They use *allude* even when whatever's referred to is clearly identified.

So our bottom-line advice is to use *allude* only in indirect reference, and to use *refer* to mean direct reference. And we'll ask you follow that advice in doing the next set of exercises.

Exercise: Allude-Refer

1. No, she didn't mention you by name, but I feel sure she was alluding/referring to you.

2. The song "My Girl Sadie" alludes/refers to the singer's sweetheart, but the poem "That Certain Someone" simply alludes/refers to the object of affection.

3. Careful speakers often avoid naming names, and simply allude/refer to those they're criticizing.

4. It may be good practice to allude/refer to the person you're praising, and to allude/refer to the object of your criticism.

5. He used the phrase "that unpleasant incident at the Christmas party" in alluding/referring to the boss's misbehavior.

6. In the beginning of his nominating speech, he made several allusions/references to the candidate before directly alluding/referring to her by name.

7. She said "You-know-who called again today," alluding/referring to the young man her daughter liked.

8. She alluded/referred to the winner by name, and alluded/referred to the others by mentioning "the admirable competitors."

9. The preacher alluded/referred to the passage, citing chapter and verse.

10. I suspect several of the men felt he was alluding/referring to them when he spoke against sins of overindulgence.

1. alluding; 2. refers, alludes; 3. allude; 4. refer, allude; 5. alluding; 6. allusions, referring; 7. alluding; 8. referred, alluded; 9. referred; 10. alluding.

Amend-Emend

If asked to pronounce these words, you'd probably make a distinct difference in their first sounds—saying *A*-mend and *EE*-mend. But, in our ordinary conversation, a lot of that difference disappears. Most people begin both words with something like an *uh* sound (a *schwa*), so they'd sound a lot alike. To add to the confusion, they overlap in meaning: if you *amend* or *emend*, you're making a change.

What kind of change? Here the road divides. A purist would say that if you *emend* something, you're removing faults. (The word comes from Latin *emendare*, to take out flaws or problems.) That same purist would say that to *amend* simply means to add something. If we revise our grocery list by changing "kauphy" to "coffee," we've *emended* the list. But if we add items, we *amend* it.

But to many people, the words mean pretty much the same thing. So who's right? As with so many questions about linguistic matters, there's no clear answer. Some people insist that the words have different meanings, while others ignore the distinction.

And where do we come down on the issue? Well, we respect both sides, but lean more toward the non-purists. One reason is history. Since the 15th century, *amend* has been used to mean "make improvements, or emend." A second reason is that many people use the words interchangeably (though *emend* is much less common).

The last reason is etymology. We gave the origin of *emend* above, so what's the origin of *amend*? It's the same. From the Latin *ex* and *mendum*, meaning removing flaws. So the fact that they come from the same source adds some credence to the idea that they can mean pretty much the same.

OUR ADVICE: Believe what you wish about these words, but behave as if you believe the purists. Don't overuse *emend*, or you'll sound stuffy. And—most importantly—remember that you don't have to use either. Our language is rich with near-synonyms, so say "improve" or "edit" or plain "fix" whenever you like.

Now we'll ask you to put on your purist's hat to do an exercise.

Exercise: Amend-Emend

1. In doing this exercise, the purist would say we're amending/emending the sentences.

2. If I want to add another item (number 11, say), I'd be amending/emending the exercise.

3. The purist would probably say that the Bill of Rights was a way to amend/emend (add to) the Constitution, not necessarily to amend/emend (improve) it.

4. After I draft this exercise, I'll send it to "She-who-must-be-obeyed" for any amendments/emendations (improvements) she'd care to make.

5. The purist wanting to make up with a friend would likely say "let's make amends/emends," rather than "let's make amends/emends."

6. This is a good list of things we'll need, but I'd like to amend/emend it with a few more items.

7. And I see that some of the items are repeated, so I'll amend/emend the list by striking them out.

8. The editor did a good job of amending/emending the text, correcting several of my typos.

9. And she amended/emended it by adding a few items I'd forgotten.

10. So, to sum up: to amend/emend is to correct or improve; to amend/emend is simply to add something.

Assume-Presume

The most-common meaning of *to assume* is to take for granted, to accept without further proof or evidence—as in "I assumed he was telling the truth."

The term has several other meanings, including to take on (to assume responsibility for a debt, to assume a role or part, to assume an office), to pretend (she assumed indifference, but she was actually disappointed), and to seize, take for oneself (he assumed control of the vessel).

To presume can also mean to take for granted, to assume without further proof (presumed innocent), and that's part of the reason these two are often interchanged—sometimes carelessly. But *presume* is in some uses a clearly stronger term, often carrying the suggestion of impetuousness, impertinent boldness. ("Sir, do you presume to tell me how I should use the language? Do you presume to speak for me and the others? You should not presume such things.")

So if you simply want to say "taken for granted," you could use *assume*. But if you want to make a stronger statement, to imply an overstepping, a going too far, you'd do better to use *presume*.

Now, may we presume to think that you're ready to assume responsibility for demonstrating your mastery of the meanings?

Exercise: Assume-Presume

1. She said "a kudo" because she assumed/presumed that the term was in standard use.

2. Although she wasn't right about that, I don't think the teacher should have assumed/presumed to lecture all of us on the need to use "kudos," which (as I assume/presume almost all of us knew) is a singular word meaning "praise."

3. I asked the young man for a menu because I assumed/presumed that he was a waiter.

4. What I had assumed/presumed was incorrect; he was the cocktail-hour piano player.

5. He seemed offended, and doubtless thought I had assumed/presumed too much.

6. I explained that what he considered my arrogant assumption/presumption was simply an incorrect but innocent assumption/presumption.

7. I assume/presume he forgave me—he came back later and smilingly brought my drink—as well as a menu.

8. So his temporary assumption/presumption that I was being presumptuous did no serious damage.

9. The scientist said that assuming/presuming something to be true without testing can be a prideful and dangerous presumption/assumption.

10. I won't assume/presume to speak with certainty, but I assume/presume that everyone did well on this exercise.

1. assumed; 2. presumed, assume; 3. assumed;
4. assumed; 5. presumed; 6. presumption, assumption; 7. assume;
8. assumption; 9. assuming, presumption; 10. presume, assume.

13

Career-Careen

In its most-common use, *career* means one's life work. ("He planned for a military career; she had a second career as a writer.") But it has another fairly common meaning—to move forward, especially at high speed. ("The runaway horse careered through the crowd.") And this sense of the word is the one that is sometimes confused with a similar term, *careen.*

Careen also means to move (often with the suggestion of high speed), but to many people it carries the idea that whatever is moving is leaning over, often lurching or swerving from side to side. ("The motorcycles careened along the winding mountain road.") The word comes from a nautical term (Latin *carina*, "ship's keel") describing a ship heeled over in a stiff breeze, or laid on its side for cleaning or repair.

But because these two words have been interchanged for many years now, it may seem stuffy or pretentious to object to this practice.

So we're not exactly objecting—we're just letting you know that many careful writers and speakers do make a distinction between these terms. But even if you careen back and forth between the two, it probably won't hurt your career.

MEMORY HOOK: Remember this rhyme—"to careen is to lean."

Exercise: Career-Careen

1. The sled careered/careened wildly back and forth as it sped down the curving trail.

2. She had trouble deciding on what to choose as a career/careen; she was always careering/careening back and forth between medicine and law.

3. When the pirate ship careered/careened straight through the blockade, the admiral was astounded, and feared that the escape might ruin his career/careen.

4. The police said that the driver had fallen asleep, and his car careered/careened straight across the cornfield.

5. The skaters careened/careered around the rink, leaving graceful, curving tracks in the ice.

6. When she was learning to ride her bicycle, she spent a good deal of time careering/careening around in wavering paths through the yard.

7. While the frightened antelopes were careering/careening wildly in zig-zag paths, the lioness careered/careened directly toward her chosen target.

8. The skiers went careering/careening among the slalom flags, while the ski-jumpers careered/careened directly down the slope.

9. The police cadets were required to career/careen through the traffic cones; if they touched too many, it might interfere with their careers/careens.

10. The drag-racers careered/careened straight down the track, while the cyclists careered/careened drunkenly in attempts to pass each other.

1. careened; 2. career, careening; 3. careered, career; 4. careered; 5. careened; 6. careening; 7. careening, careered; 8. careening, careered; 9. career, careers; 10. careered, careened.

Canvas-Canvass

These two words are pronounced the same, so the difference is in spelling—one little letter, more or less, makes the difference. The terms are used just often enough so that we should know which is which, but not quite often enough to make that easy to remember.

Canvas is a heavy, durable cloth or fabric used for ground cover, heavy tote bags, rough-use clothing, furniture cover, tarps, and the like.

To *canvass*, in common usage, means to solicit votes, opinions, subscriptions, donations, etc., often by going house to house, or polling members of a specific group. ("The pollsters canvassed the neighborhood, asking people in the 18–25 age group how they planned to vote.") The term can also mean to examine carefully, to vet thoroughly.

So here's a little quiz to vet your knowledge of the difference between these two words.

Exercise: Canvas-Canvass

1. When the entomologist went into the forest to canvas/canvass the natives about their knowledge of local insects, she wore her canvas/canvass jacket.

2. Pollsters must plan carefully if they want the results of a canvas/canvass to be accurate.

3. Lister bags made of canvas/canvass let some of the drinking water seep through and evaporate, keeping the liquid cool.

4. The detective brought in a canvas/canvass bag containing the evidence, which he asked the analyst to canvas/canvass carefully for any fingerprints or traces of blood.

5. The campground host will canvas/canvass the people at each site to see if they need pieces of canvas/canvass to put under their tents.

6. The navy historian decided to canvas/canvass the old sailors to see if any remembered boats using sails made of canvas/canvass.

7. The teacher liked to canvas/canvass his students from time to time, to see which words they were interested in learning.

8. We will canvas/canvass the drivers at the truck stop to see what percentage of them use canvas/canvass covers for the goods they haul.

9. The pollsters will canvas/canvass people in the over-fifty demographic about their eating habits.

10. The clothing manufacturers will canvas/canvass area blacksmiths to see how many wear canvas/canvass gloves.

1. canvass, canvas; 2. canvass; 3. canvas; 4. canvas, canvass; 5. canvass, canvas; 6. canvass, canvas; 7. canvass; 8. canvass, canvas; 9. canvass; 10. canvass, canvas.

Cumulative Exercise:
Aid-Aide, Allude-Refer,
Amend-Emend

1. She decided to aid/aide the family by getting a job as a nurse's aid/aide.

2. She didn't allude/refer to anyone by name, but discreetly alluded/referred to the need for "a certain relative" to amend/emend his behavior.

3. She served a stint as an aid/aide to a senior officer, which could aid/aide her career.

4. The professor said that a student could aid/aide his grade by using fewer vague allusions/references, and instead clearly citing sources, alluding/referring to the author, title, and page.

5. He also told them he wanted quality, not quantity—so in rewriting, they should make amendments/emendations, not amendments/emendations.

6. I'm not sure, but he may have been alluding/referring to my paper, which I knew I should have amended/emended before turning it in.

1. aid, aide; 2. refer, alluded, emend; 3. aide, aid; 4. aid, allusions, referring; 5. emendations, amendments; 6. alluding, emended.

18

Cumulative Exercise:
Assume-Presume, Careen-Career,
Canvas-Canvass

1. I'm inclined to assume/presume that he was alluding to us, but we don't want to assume/presume too much, too soon.

2. If I careen/career headlong into that sticky debate, it may hurt my careen/career.

3. We should first canvas/canvass our friends, instead of assuming/presuming to know what they think.

4. The little sailboats careened/careered back and forth into the wind; the powerboat careened/careered directly across the lake.

5. It's not always easy to know when you're making a reasonable assumption/presumption, and when you're making a premature assumption/presumption.

6. But let's assume/presume, for the sake of argument, that results of the canvas/canvass are favorable.

7. The reporter was assuming/presuming too much. The TARP is an economic-recovery program; it has nothing to do with a canvas/canvass cover.

8. I won't assume/presume to tell him how to do his job, but he shouldn't always assume/presume that he's right.

9. He tends to careen/career straight through a complex question, instead of canvasing/canvassing people who are qualified to advise him.

1. assume, presume; 2. career, career; 3. canvass, presuming; 4. careened, careered; 5. assumption, presumption; 6. assume, canvass; 7. presuming, canvas; 8. presume, assume; 9. career, canvassing.

Care for a Bunch of Carats-Carets-Karats-Carrots?

It's not often that we have four separate words that sound alike, but this quartet manages it. We'll give you their meanings, and then some memory hooks to hang them on.

First, the meanings:

A *carat* is a unit of weight for precious stones. A *caret* (^) is the little up-pointing proofreader's "insert" mark. A *karat* is a measure of the fineness of gold. And *carrots* are what rabbits eat.

And now for your memory hooks:

For the one that begins with "k," think "The inscription 14 K means fourteen Karat gold" (or Ken is A RAT because he gave me no gold).

For *carat*, the word that's used for precious stones, here's a quote to remind yourself of the beginning and end of the word: "C my new diamond ring—I bought it AT Tiffany's."

For the proofreader's mark, we all know that *et* means "and"—as in "Et tu, Brute" and "et al" (and others). That will help us remember that a carET means "*and* something"—a letter or such—should be added where you see the mark.

And for the one that ends in "ot," think of a plate of carrots On the Table.

NOTE: Some dictionaries list the words for gold (karat) and precious stones (carat) as variant forms of each other, so they are sometimes interchanged—but we recommend that you keep them separate in your own writing.

Exercise: Carats-Carets-Karats-Carrots?

1. The Hope diamond, the world's largest blue diamond, weighs 44.5 karats/carats/carets.

2. The applicant taking a test for the proofreader's job should not have penned in a karat/carat/caret and apostrophe with the *its* in "Every dog has its day."

3. While digging up some karats/carats/carets/carrots in her garden, she unearthed the 24-karat/carat/caret gold ring she'd lost the previous year.

4. The ring had a 1.5 karat/carat/caret sapphire mounted between smaller stones.

5. The editor uses karats/carats/carets to show where something should be added.

6. When she found his shopping list, she smiled and used a karat/carat/caret to insert "And a 24-karat/carat/caret gold ring for your dear wife, inset with a two-karat/carat/caret emerald."

7. Good proofreaders take special care with their karats/carats/carets.

8. Twenty-four-karat/carat/caret gold is exceedingly fine.

9. Precious stones are usually measured in karats/carats/carets; the fineness of gold is given in karats/carats/carets.

10. Goldsmiths measure in karats/carats/carets; proofreaders and editors use karats/carats/carets; cooks carefully consider their karats/carats/carets/carrots.

1. carats; 2. caret; 3. carrots, karat; 4. carat; 5. carets; 6. caret, karat, carat; 7. carets; 8. karat; 9. carats, karats; 10. karats, carets, carrots.

21

Censure-Censor-Sensor-Censer

As we said about the bunch of carrots, it's rare to have four words that sound alike. But here's another quartet that almost makes the cut. (Three out of four are homophones, and censure has a similar, but not identical, sound.)

Censure is a verb meaning to criticize harshly, to show strong disapproval, or to officially reprimand a member of a group (especially a legislator). "They voted to censure the senator who had been caught selling pornography from his office." The word can also be a noun, meaning the criticism itself: "The censure from the media was nearly unanimous."

A *censor* is a person who evaluates such things as movies, radio and TV programs, books and magazines, for the purpose of identifying parts considered inappropriate or objectionable. "In wartime, the military appoints censors to delete (censor) parts of letters, emails, and other communications considered possible security breaches."

A *sensor* is a device that detects (or senses) levels of light, radiation, electronic signals, etc. "NASA puts remote sensors on some satellites." "The security light uses motion-detecting sensors." "Catfish have delicate sensors to detect food." As a memory hook, you can use the word's similarity to *sense*.

And a *censer* is a container holding burning incense—especially the kind swung on a chain during religious services. "The children were amazed when the priest swung the smoking censer back and forth as he uttered phrases they could not understand."

Pronunciation: Sensor, censor, and censer are pronounced pretty much the same—making a fairly close rhyme with fencer. But censure is different; it gets a sh sound, as in sugar. So think SIN-SURE—"If the church official finds out about a sin, the sinner would surely get censured."

If you're sensitive, your internal sensors may have sensed that there's an exercise coming up—an uncensored one.

Exercise: Censure-Censor-Sensor-Censer

1. We're pleased that the publisher's censure/censor/sensor/censer didn't delete (censure/censor/sensor/censer) this exercise.

2. At the First Church of Goodness and Mercy, they do not censure/censor/sensor/censer members for minor sins, nor do they swing censures/censors/sensors/censers during the service.

3. During WWII, the telegrams from servicemen were often censured/censored/sensored/censered.

4. The detective planted remote censures/censors/sensors/censers in the suspect's room.

5. In the review, her new play was cruelly censured/censored/sensored/censered by the watchdog organization's censure/censor/sensor/censer.

6. Plants have light-sensitive censures/censors/sensors/censers that influence the way they grow.

7. The nose is a censure/censor/sensor/censer that senses the scent from the censure/censor/sensor/censer during the services.

8. During her career as a censure/censor/sensor/censer for children's books, she suggested revisions, but rarely gave an outright censure/censor/sensor/censer to a story.

9. The wizard swung a censure/censor/sensor/censer back and forth as he muttered incantations.

10. If the mental censure/censor/sensor/censer of the straight-laced censure/censor/sensor/censer senses pornography, he'll surely write a scathing review to censure/censor/sensor/censer the writer's work.

1. censor, censor; 2. censure, censers; 3. censored; 4. sensors; 5. censured, censor; 6. sensors; 7. sensor, censer; 8. censor, censure; 9. censer; 10. sensor, censor, censure.

Childish-Childlike

These two look-alikes have something in common—both are used to describe adult behavior (or attitude) that we might expect of a child. But one of the words almost always has a fairly strong negative connotation, while the other is most often used in a positive sense.

To say that something or someone is *childish* is to criticize, to suggest silliness, immaturity, or lack of judgment. "I'm tired of his childish, infantile tantrums." (A slightly fancier word meaning much the same thing is puerile—pronounced PYOO-ur-ill.)

But *childlike* normally carries no such negative charge. In fact, it's often intended as something of a compliment, as in "He was moved by the wide-eyed wonder and childlike innocence of the villagers who came to see the magic show."

Of course, innocence is sometimes associated with ignorance, lack of wisdom, unawareness of how the world works—so be careful. If you do want a word that includes a negative element, one that's slightly critical, you can use naive (nah-EVE).

And here's a memory hook for you: One way to remember the difference between these words is that childLIKE usually refers to something we LIKE. So in childlike innocence, we offer you this humble quiz, and hope you won't have a childish tantrum if you don't ace it.

Exercise: Childish-Childlike

1. We thought he was mature and reasonable, until we saw his childlike/childish display of temper.

2. The wide-eyed openness and childlike/childish expression on the poor woman's face touched our hearts.

3. The con man tried to put on a display of childlike/childish innocence, but only succeeded in coming across as childlike/childish.

4. The player made no friends among the reporters with his childlike/childish tantrum after failing to score.

5. Chris liked the childlike/childish purity of the youngsters' faces.

6. But Lee thought Chris was being childlike/childish and overly sentimental.

7. Pat thought it was childlike/childish of the art student to pout because his painting of animals with appealing, childlike/childish features was not awarded a prize.

8. My friend didn't like the play—he considered the acting childlike/childish.

9. But to me it seemed refreshingly childlike/childish and unpretentious.

10. Too often, youngsters seem to go from engaging, childlike/childish innocence directly to exasperating, childlike/childish behavior.

1. childish; 2. childlike; 3. childlike; childish; 4. childish; 5. childlike; 6. childish; 7. childish, childlike; 8. childish; 9. childlike; 10. childlike, childish.

25

Demur-Demure

These words look and sound a good deal alike—that's part of the reason they are often unintentionally interchanged. They also share a little commonality in meaning, which adds to an even greater likelihood that they'll be mixed up. But if you pay attention to the slight difference in spelling and pronunciation, you'll be able to avoid confusion.

To *demur* (rhymes with *refer*) means to decline to do something, to pause, to hesitate. The word is not usually used to mean an abrupt refusal, but is more likely to be used when someone gently and politely declines some sort or suggestion or offer. "He asked her to accompany him on his cruise, but she demurred."

Demure means shy, modest, proper in behavior—often in a coy, playful, or deceptive way. "Oh no," she answered demurely, "surely you don't think I'd even consider skinny-dipping." But her sly smile hinted that she might.

We hope you won't demurely demur when we invite you take the following quiz.

Exercise: Demur-Demure

1. She looked demur/demure, but did not demur/demure for a second when invited to leap into the mosh pit.

2. The painter worked hard to capture the demur/demure expression on the model's face.

3. When asked to give a direct answer to the question, the candidate said he'd have to demur/demure.

4. A demur/demure smile sometimes turneth away wrath.

5. The shy guy usually demurred/demured when invited to join in the games.

6. In that era, girls were taught to behave in a demur/demure fashion.

7. The advice of the life coach was: Don't demur/demure; do it today.

8. If you're too demur/demure, you may not have as many offers to demur/demure from.

9. Auntie Mame said she wasn't interested in being demur/demure, and she wasn't in the habit of demuring/demurring from an interesting offer.

10. When opportunity knocks, don't try to act demur/demure, and don't demur/demure too long.

1. demure, demur; 2. demure; 3. demur; 4. demure; 5. demurred; 6. demure; 7. demur; 8. demure, demur; 9. demure, demurring; 10. demure, demur.

Discreet-Discrete

Discreet means judicious in speech or behavior, especially about respecting someone else's privacy, or about a topic of a delicate nature. "I'm sure the mayor wouldn't use an office computer to send emails to his paramour; he's much too discreet."

Discrete means separate, distinct, or detached—"The mass, which appeared to be one solid glob, was on closer inspection found to be made up of hundreds of discrete insects, clinging together around their queen."

How can we remember which is which? They are pronounced the same, which can add to the confusion. But the spelling is different—each of these words is an anagram of the other—they use the same letters, just in different arrangements. And that difference provides our hook.

Each word has two "e's." But in the word *discrete*, the "e's" are separated by another letter. And as we've said, things that are discrete are separate—distinct from each other and from their surroundings. The word with the "e's" separated is the one that means separate, distinct.

In the word *discreet*, the "e's" are side by side. Remember that someone who's discreet is prudent, respects privacy, and keeps silent about anything delicate or secret. Picture two people putting their heads together (like the "e's" in *discreet*) to talk privately.

And now you have your memory hook. The two "e's" in *discrete* (meaning separate) are separate from each other, with a "t" between them. But the "e's" in *discreet* are together, like the heads of two people discreetly whispering secrets.

Here are ten discrete items to check your understanding. If we learn that you didn't get them all right, we'll be too discreet to reveal that fact to anyone else.

Exercise: Discreet-Discrete

1. Hawaii is an archipelago, made up of several discreet/discrete islands.

2. The young lovers were seen discretely/discreetly whispering to each other on three discreet/discrete occasions.

3. A canoe has one hull, but a catamaran has two discreet/discrete hulls.

4. What appear to be three discreet/discrete islands are really three mounds of an underwater reef.

5. After I'd given my oral report, the professor discreetly/discretely told me that the Portuguese man-of-war is not a single animal, as I'd said, but a colony of four somewhat discreet/discrete individuals.

6. A glissando played on a piano, unlike that played on a violin, is really made up of very short but discreet/discrete notes.

7. A supervisor should be discreet/discrete when discussing an employee's personal problems.

8. The counselor told Liz that she had behaved indiscreetly/indiscretely on several discreet/discrete occasions.

9. She said that she'd love to meet him, but that they'd have to be discreet/discrete.

10. At several discreet/discrete meetings, he has rushed in and acted too quickly; he should learn to be more discreet/discrete.

1. discrete; 2. discreetly, discrete; 3. discrete; 4. discrete; 5. discreetly, discrete; 6. discrete; 7. discreet; 8. indiscreetly, discrete; 9. discrete; 10. discrete, discreet.

Disinterested-Uninterested

As we said elsewhere, there's nothing wrong with an informed opinion, as long as it's identified as such. So here's our opinion—and our advice—about *disinterested* and *uninterested*.

Use *disinterested* when you mean something like "lack of selfish or personal interest in the matter or its outcome." So you'd want a trial judge, a referee, or a scientific researcher to be *disinterested*—even though they're likely very interested in the events they're evaluating.

Uninterested expresses unconcern, a lack of any kind of interest. Use it when you're talking about someone who just doesn't care one way or the other. "The person who never turns on the TV is uninterested in what the channels have to offer." "The person who never listens to any kind of music is uninterested in that art form."

We expect the baseball umpire to be *disinterested*, but would guess that the person who politely refuses a free ticket to the game is *uninterested*.

Of course people don't always follow advice about usage. (Maybe they're uninterested.) That's understandable—the blurring and overlap in meanings of these two words has been going on for a long time. But even though some good writers and speakers interchange these words, most careful writers and editors do make a distinction between them. So it would be a good idea to observe the difference in your own speaking and (especially) writing, but try to accept the fact that not everybody will agree with your way of doing it.

We can't say that we're uninterested in how well you do on the following exercises, but if we were grading your paper, we'd try to be disinterested.

Exercise: Disinterested-Uninterested

1. The detective sent the DNA sample to the lab to be examined by an expert who was disinterested/uninterested.

2. She doesn't care about the game. But even though she's disinterested/uninterested, she knows the rules. So she'd be a good, disinterested/uninterested observer.

3. The judge recused himself on the grounds that he could not honestly say that he was disinterested/uninterested in the outcome.

4. As a girl she seemed disinterested/uninterested in dancing, but later became an avid participant.

5. Nobody who's disinterested/uninterested in science is likely to become a forensic analyst.

6. But every forensic analyst should be disinterested/uninterested in the results of an analysis.

7. We can't expect teachers to be disinterested/uninterested in the exam results, but, when scoring the papers, they should definitely try to be disinterested/uninterested.

8. The person who falls asleep during the play is probably disinterested/uninterested; the critic who evaluates the acting should be disinterested/uninterested.

9. A good marriage counselor should be disinterested/uninterested in the personalities of the couple.

10. The editorial complained that the party-line voting records of the Supreme Court justices proved that they were not all as disinterested/uninterested as they should have been.

1. disinterested; 2. uninterested, disinterested; 3. disinterested; 4. uninterested; 5. uninterested; 6. disinterested; 7. uninterested, disinterested; 8. uninterested, disinterested; 9. disinterested; 10. disinterested.

Cumulative Exercise:
Carats-Carets-Karats-Carrots,
Censure-Censor-Sensor-Censer,
Childlike-Childish

1. She harshly censured/censored/sensored his behavior, saying his actions were childlike/childish.

2. The jewel weighed several carats/karats/carets, and it was mounted in a band of 14-carat/karat/caret gold.

3. The teacher was moved by the childlike/childish innocence of the student, but irritated by the childlike/childish tantrum of his classmate.

4. As a figurative carat/caret/karat/carrot on a stick, the teacher promised one point for each correct use of the carat/caret/karat/carrot to mark insertions.

5. The morality committee members strongly criticized (censured/censored/sensored) the author of the children's book, then they censered/censored/censured the draft, deleting some words and phrases, and using carats/carets/karats/carrots to insert euphemisms.

6. It was foolish, even childlike/childish, of him to believe the street-vendor's claim that the ruby weighed thirty carats/carets/karats/carrots, and that the earrings were 24-carat/caret/karat/carrot gold.

1. censured, childish; 2. carats, karat; 3. childlike, childish; 4. carrot, caret;
5. censured, censored, carets; 6. childish, carats, karat.

32

Cumulative Exercise:
Demur-Demure, Discreet-Discrete,
Disinterested-Uninterested

1. As we've learned, some words have several discreet/discrete meanings.

2. She was invited to judge the debate, but had to demur/demure, explaining that she had friends on one team and so could not be disinterested/uninterested in the outcome.

3. He invited her to the playoffs, but she said she'd demur/demure.

4. Later, she discreetly/discretely whispered that she was disinterested/uninterested in team sports, but might consider a game of singles.

5. What appeared to be a solid sphere turned out to be made up of thousands of discreet/discrete frog eggs clinging together.

6. Considering me an observer who was disinterested/uninterested in who won, the player nearest me asked if I thought the ball had gone out of bounds.

7. But I had to demur/demure, thinking it would be indiscreet/indiscrete to refute the other player's call.

8. As someone who's disinterested/uninterested in the scientists' debate, do you think time flows in a steady stream, or that it's made up of discreet/discrete instants?

9. She was very demur/demure and discreet/discrete; she would demur/demure from giving an opinion when she didn't feel she could truly consider herself disinterested/uninterested.

1. discrete; 2. demur, disinterested; 3. demur; 4. discreetly, uninterested; 5. discrete; 6. disinterested; 7. demur, indiscreet; 8. disinterested, discrete; 9. demure, discreet, demur, disinterested.

Disassemble-Dissemble

People who are careful of their enunciation—who clearly pronounce the "a" in *disassemble*—are probably less likely to mix these two words up. And they're almost certainly less likely to confuse their listeners about which word they mean.

Here's the difference: *Disassemble* means to take apart—the opposite of assemble. It's a fairly simple, straightforward word, with a clear meaning. "The instructor demonstrated the proper way to disassemble the motor."

But *dissemble* is more complex (and is not used as often). It means to speak or behave so as to intentionally mislead, to give a false or misleading impression, to act hypocritically and somewhat dishonestly. "The child was dissembling when he said, with apparent innocence, that he didn't intend to pull his sister's hair." (It's pronounced dis-EM-b'l.)

Exercise: Disassemble-Dissemble

1. Sometimes you can get a clue to the meaning of a word if you disassemble/dissemble it—looking at the root and any prefix or suffix.

2. The lobbyist was disassembling/dissembling when he said he was concerned only about the welfare of the residents, not about the money he'd make.

3. I'm beginning to believe that the salesman disassembled/dissembled when he assured me that the device would be easy to disassemble/dissemble.

4. "Moi?" she said in mock disbelief. "Do you think I'd stoop to disassembling/dissembling about my true motives?"

5. The politicians were clearly disassembling/dissembling when they made such misleading statements.

6. As soon as they got themselves elected, they began working to disassemble/dissemble the programs they had promised to expand.

7. People who disassemble/dissemble may unknowingly be disassembling/dissembling their reputations.

8. The drill instructor wasn't disassembling/dissembling; he really could disassemble/dissemble the weapon and put it back together in less than thirty seconds.

9. The skeptical IRS agent suspected that the taxpayer was disassembling/dissembling.

10. Some greedy politicians and so-called spiritual leaders make a career of disassembling/dissembling.

1. disassemble; 2. dissembling; 3. dissembled, disassemble; 4. dissembling; 5. dissembling; 6. disassemble; 7. dissemble, disassembling; 8. dissembling, disassemble; 9. dissembling; 10. dissembling.

Elicit-Illicit

Elicit (ee-LISS-it) means to draw out, bring out, as in "She kept asking questions, hoping to elicit responses from her students." The word is based on Latin *ex* (out) and a root meaning to lure, entice.

Illicit, on the other hand, means unlawful, unlicensed, unauthorized. (The word is pronounced ill-ISS-it.) The prefix here is *in* (meaning *not*), which has been changed to *il* to match the beginning of the root *licit*—meaning lawful. (This type of match-up change is called assimilation.)

Of course, a word can mean different things to different people, in different subjects or different contexts. It's interesting that in linguistics, *illicit* may mean ungrammatical or improperly formed.

Although many people are careful to pronounce these words differently (especially in any kind of formal or business setting), many of us don't make a clear distinction—especially in casual conversation. It's not rare to hear educated speakers say something like *ullicit* for either term.

We generally accept such approximate pronunciations. But it's a good idea—especially in writing—to make sure you're using the word that matches your meaning.

So we'll elicit your responses to the quiz items on the next page, and hope that you don't do anything linguistically illicit.

Exercise: Elicit-Illicit

1. The lawyer asked clever questions, hoping to elicit/illicit answers that proved the defendant had done something elicit/illicit.

2. The officer said that it was elicit/illicit to elicit/illicit contributions from employees.

3. The conductor bent forward, piercing the air with his baton in an attempt to elicit/illicit the desired sounds from the orchestra.

4. Undercover narcotics investigators work hard to elicit/illicit information about elicit/illicit drug activity.

5. As a linguistics teacher, she tried to elicit/illicit responses that would help her students see how to avoid elicit/illicit verbal constructions.

6. A detective who goes too far in trying to elicit/illicit information about elicit/illicit activities may be guilty of entrapment, which is itself an elicit/illicit act.

7. Sometimes there's a fine line between eliciting/illiciting (which is often legal) and soliciting (which can be elicit/illicit).

8. His hard-luck story was intended to elicit/illicit pity, and perhaps a donation.

9. That may have been okay, if he hadn't displayed an elicit/illicit certificate of disability.

10. Touting his elicit/illicit pyramid scheme, he was able to elicit/illicit lots of money from duped investors.

1. elicit, illicit; 2. illicit, elicit; 3. elicit; 4. elicit, illicit; 5. elicit, illicit; 6. elicit, illicit, illicit; 7. eliciting, illicit; 8. elicit; 9. illicit; 10. illicit, elicit.

37

Faze-Phase

These words have an interesting history. *Faze* is an American variant of an older verb *feeze*. And those two aren't the only spellings this word has gone through. One reference says the term was spelled in about a dozen different ways, and another writer said that the word held the unique position of being the only word in the English language that would be impossible to misspell, no matter how hard we try, because of the many variant spellings.

Although we still run across variant spellings occasionally, *faze* is by far the most common, and—in most references—the standard form of the word meaning to discourage, daunt, disconcert. It's usually used in the negative, as "It didn't faze him, nothing fazes him, don't let it faze you." And even if some people consider *phase* a legitimate variant form of *faze*, its use in that sense is rare (or at least highly unusual) among careful speakers and writers.

Now for *phase*. In its most common use, *phase* is a noun meaning a distinct stage of development, a stage in an ongoing process of change. But it's also used as a verb, as in "to phase in, phase out." The sense here is to start, or bring to an end, gradually. *Phase* can also mean to put in order, to coordinate, to synchronize.

So to sum up: The standard use of *faze* is to daunt, discourage, disconcert, dishearten. And *phase* is the standard form for the word meaning "stage in a process of development," or "phase in/out."

Here's a memory hook: mentally link the F in *faze* to Frighten. (It didn't frighten/faze her at all.) And of course you could use the first letter of *phase* to help remember that it often refers to one stage in a Process.

Our next phase is the following exercise, which we hope won't faze you.

Exercise: Faze-Phase

1. We'll gradually faze/phase out the old models as the new ones are introduced.

2. Don't let his behavior faze/phase you; he's just going through a faze/phase.

3. He told the children that there might be werewolves at this faze/phase of the moon, but it didn't seem to faze/phase them.

4. At this faze/phase in the development of the Dobson fly, it has huge, tusk-like pincers.

5. He went cheerfully through every faze/phase of the initiation.

6. Even the hazing didn't seem to faze/phase him.

7. She aced the geometry exams, but the next faze/phase of the curriculum, which included differential calculus, did faze/phase her a bit.

8. The chairman of the math department, unfazed/unphased by the advent of new technology, decided to faze/phase out the slide rule and faze/phase in the electronic devices.

9. I can't say I'm unfazed/unphased by the way the electronic dictionaries and websites are causing publishers to faze/phase out our old print-on-paper friends.

10. Each faze/phase of life presents us with challenges which might faze/phase us to some degree.

1. phase; 2. faze, phase; 3. phase, faze; 4. phase; 5. phase; 6. faze; 7. phase, faze; 8. unfazed, phase, phase; 9. unfazed, phase; 10. phase, faze.

Flair-Flare

Most people pronounce these words pretty much the same—or so nearly alike that it's hard to tell which one is meant. Of course there's that spelling difference, which means that we have to be careful in writing the words, to make sure we're using the one intended.

Flair means a natural talent or ability—as in a flair for making entertaining talks, or writing songs, or painting. It can also mean elegance, style—"She always entertained her guests with flair."

A *flare* is a lighted signal, like the warning flares to alert drivers of a problem ahead. As a verb, it can mean to spread or curve away from center—"The polka-dancer's skirt flared outward as she spun around the floor."

A mnemonic? One way to remember is that a *flare* means motorists should take CARE, while *flair* ends with the same -AIR spelling as debonAIR.

With that in mind as you do the following exercise, don't just work through it—attack it with flair.

Exercise: Flair-Flare

1. The blacksmith used a cone-shaped tool to flair/flare out the end of the tube.

2. The fireworks flaired/flared out brightly in the evening sky.

3. The boys' drill-team performed with flair/flare, wearing bell-bottoms that flaired/flared out around their ankles.

4. The sheriff instructed his deputies to flair/flare out and search the area.

5. Her speech was not only well written; it was also delivered with flair/flare.

6. Magus the magician performed with flair/flare, juggling burning flares/flairs.

7. Winton inserted a mute into the flared/flaired end of his trumpet.

8. He then played the "Carmen Fantasia" with his usual flair/flare.

9. As the wasps flared/flaired out from the nest he'd disturbed, he leaped the fence with flair/flare and dashed away.

10. The way you're working this quiz shows that you have a flair/flare for language.

1. flare; 2. flared; 3. flair, flared; 4. flare; 5. flair; 6. flair, flares; 7. flared; 8. flair; 9. flared, flair; 10. flair.

Gantlet-Gauntlet

For years (from the 19th century to the mid 20th), our dictionaries told us that we should say "run the gantlet" and "throw down the gauntlet." By their definitions, a *gantlet* was two lines or rows of something. The phrase "run the gantlet" referred to a punishment in which an offender had to run between two rows of people (often soldiers holding sticks or whips) who struck him as he passed. (A milder variation is the belt-line.) Among people interested in trains and railroads, *gantlet* refers to two sets of railroad tracks that run alongside each other.

A *gauntlet* was defined as a glove—especially a glove with a long, protective sheath that covered the wrist. Gauntlets were worn by people (like welders) who worked with hot things, and by knights and other fighting men. To throw down the gauntlet was to issue a challenge, as to a duel.

We accepted and followed the dictionaries' advice, but later learned that things are a bit more complicated. The term used in the running punishment came from the English word *gantlope*, which itself came from a Swedish term. The word morphed into *gauntlet* through a process known as folk etymology, where a more-common word (*gauntlet* in this case) is used for a newer or less-familiar one.

So if you're talking about the running punishment, either is okay; both are considered standard. If you're talking about a railroad-track arrangement (or something similar), we recommend you use *gantlet*. But a glove, on the other hand, is pretty much always a *gauntlet*.

On the *other* other hand, there's the question of majority opinion, of more-common usage. If you care about such things, you may want to go with "run the gauntlet." It's said to be the more-common spelling. (A Google check came up with 226,000 hits for "run the gauntlet," and just 35,000 for "run the gantlet.") But a recent article in *Smithsonian* magazine described seals running a gantlet of hungry sharks. So it really is your choice.

We won't throw down a gauntlet, or ask you to run a gantlet; we'll just give you this little exercise.

Exercise: Gantlet-Gauntlet

1. I'd rather someone throw down the gauntlet/gantlet/either than to throw a shoe at me.

2. The highway patrol had set up a gauntlet/gantlet/either of traffic cones to funnel the cars through.

3. My train slowed as it passed through the gauntlet/gantlet/either of tracks.

4. I noticed that the railroad workers wore gauntlets/gantlets/either with heavy cuffs.

5. Tired of Fast Freddy's bragging about his pool skill, Bill threw down the gauntlet/gantlet/either, challenging him to a match.

6. In some of the boys' clubs, the initiation included a running of the gauntlet/gantlet/either.

7. The bride and groom left the church through a gauntlet/gantlet/either of their well-wishers, who lined both sides of the steps.

8. To keep our forearms from being heavily scratched, we wore gauntlets/gantlets/either while trimming the brush.

9. The young men of the tribe had to run a gauntlet/gantlet/either of elders, who swatted them with switches as they passed.

10. The two rows of thorny bushes formed a gauntlet/gantlet/either that the hikers had to pass through.

1. gauntlet; 2. gantlet; 3. gantlet; 4. gauntlets; 5. gauntlet; 6. either; 7. gantlet; 8. gauntlets; 9. either; 10. gantlet.

Hoard-Horde

Here's another double-trouble pair. Not only do most people pronounce them pretty much the same (to rhyme with board), but—although they are definitely two different terms—the words also have some slight overlap in meaning.

Horde is probably the simpler one, so let's look at it first. It's a noun, meaning a multitude of people or things: "The nomadic horde would swoop down on villages, plundering and pillaging, " or "Sneadly always had a horde of complaints—about his work, his boss, and his love life." It often, but not always, has a negative connotation.

Hoard can be either a verb or a noun. As a verb, it means to save up, to stash, as for an emergency: "Some people, when worried about the stock market, will begin to hoard gold."

As a noun, *hoard* means the stash itself—the cache of collected or saved-up stuff. "Fortunato was busy building a hoard of silver; his studious and poetic sister developed an impressive word-hoard."

Here are a few questions—not enough to make a horde—to see if you've hoarded enough information about these two terms.

Exercise: Hoard-Horde

1. For years the Mongol hoards/hordes tormented the residents, making sudden, vicious attacks.

2. If any of the villagers had put away a hoard/horde of supplies, the Mongols were sure to find it.

3. The treasure hunters trekked through the jungle, hoping to discover the rumored hoard/horde of gold and gems.

4. As they entered the swamp, a hoard/horde of mosquitoes descended on them.

5. Selfish people will sometimes hoard/horde things they should share with others.

6. She's a benevolent hoarder/horder; her cache consists of good books.

7. Just as they finished putting away their hoard/horde of supplies for the winter, a hoard/horde of pirates swarmed in and stole it.

8. The Viking chief, proud of his clan, opened up his word-hoard/word-horde and praised their behavior.

9. Scrooge complained bitterly about the hoard/horde of beggars, even as he hoarded/horded money until he had a huge hoard/horde.

10. The farmer's wife hoarded/horded the eggs until she had quite a hoard/horde stashed away in the incubator. When they hatched, a hoard/horde of young chicks swarmed from the chicken house out into the barnyard.

1. hordes; 2. hoard; 3. hoard; 4. horde; 5. hoard; 6. hoarder;
7. hoard, horde; 8. word-hoard; 9. horde, hoarded, hoard;
10. hoarded, hoard, horde.

45

Cumulative Exercise:
Disassemble-Dissemble, Elicit-Illicit, Faze-Phase

1. Unfazed/Unphased by the danger, the corporal coolly disassembled/dissembled the explosive device.

2. His skill elicited/illicited praise from the onlookers.

3. I'm sure the politician was disassembling/dissembling when he asked, with a childlike expression on his face, "Is it elicit/illicit to solicit donations from lobbyists?"

4. At that faze/phase of his career, he discreetly elicited/illicited aid from several discrete organizations.

5. The governor seemed unfazed/unphased by the charge that he had disassembled/dissembled in claiming that he had not knowingly done anything elicit/illicit.

6. He was accused of such elicit/illicit actions as eliciting/illiciting contributions in exchange for political favors.

7. By continuing to disassemble/dissemble, he was unknowingly disassembling/dissembling the base of his support among voters.

8. The final faze/phase of the scandal came when he disassembled/dissembled the competent team his predecessor had recruited.

9. In a clear demonstration of how unfazed/unphased he was by the accusations, he continued to disassemble/dissemble and mislead, trying to elicit/illicit sympathy from those he had lied to.

9. unfazed, dissemble, elicit.
7. dissemble, disassembling; 8. phase, disassembled;
4. phase, elicited; 5. unfazed, dissembled, illicit; 6. illicit, eliciting;
1. Unfazed, disassembled; 2. elicited; 3. dissembling, illicit;

46

Cumulative Exercise: Flair-Flare, Gantlet-Gauntlet, Hoard-Horde

1. The article mistakenly said the designer "had a flair/flare" for creating fashionable gowns; it should have said flare/flair.

2. The tourists walked through a gantlet/gauntlet/either of people peddling their wares.

3. A hoard/horde of insects swarmed about the trekkers; a guide lit a flair/flare to dispel them.

4. The beekeeper pulled on a pair of gantlets/gauntlets/either, then set to work with a certain stylish flair/flare.

5. The student drivers had to maneuver through a gantlet/gauntlet/either of traffic cones.

6. The patrolman, who wore a Smoky-Bear hat and a pair of gantlets/gauntlets/either, gave a driving demonstration.

7. After explaining that the gantlets/gauntlets/either protected him from burns when he lit highway flairs/flares, he guided his cruiser through the gantlet/gauntlet/either with flair/flare.

8. The grizzled old miser hoarded/horded his money, even though he had hoards/hordes of sheep and cattle that brought him a large and steady income.

9. A hoard/horde of gazelles swept across the prairie, careening back and forth with flair/flare.

1. flare, flair; 2. either*; 3. horde, flare*; 4. gauntlets, flair; 5. gantlet; 6. gauntlets; 7. gauntlets, flares, gantlet, flair 8. hoarded, hordes; 9. horde, flair.

47

Liable-Libel

One problem with these words is that some people tend to pronounce them nearly alike (usually LIE-b'l, which is standard for *libel*). The standard pronunciation of *liable* gives it three syllables— LIE-uh-b'l.

Libel is mainly a legal term. A good working definition is "written slander." A longer and more formal one is "defamation or damage to someone's reputation or well being through publication of words, pictures, or other graphic means." The word *libel* can also be used as a verb—as in "The amoral politician would libel his enemies if he thought he could get away with it."

Liable is a little more complex, with more uses. One of the most common meanings is "legally responsible, or subject to legal action"— as in "If you do that, you may be liable for damages."

Another is "at risk of having something happen," and that something is almost always unpleasant or undesirable: "If he climbs that wall, he's liable to fall and hurt himself." In this sense, it means much the same as *apt* or *likely*.

If you're careful with your pronunciation of these two words, you're not liable to misspell either, nor to have your listeners question your knowledge of the difference.

Exercise: Liable-Libel

1. If you're not careful what you say in your email, you may be liable/libel for liable/libel.

2. And if you aren't careful with your choice of confusing words, you're liable/libel to be misunderstood.

3. Even famous journalists and broadcasters are sometimes sued for liable/libel.

4. If they harm someone's reputation, they may be liable/libel for damages.

5. Even though she knew the difference, when tired she was liable/libel to write "it's" when she meant "its."

6. The judge ruled that the manufacturer was liable/libel for damages caused by the product.

7. Journalism classes include a section on the kinds of writing that can make the author liable/libel for liable/libel.

8. A soft answer can not only turneth away wrath, it may also turneth away a liable/libel suit.

9. A writer who liables/libels someone is liable/libel to be charged with liable/libel.

10. Now that I've completed the exercise, I'm not liable/libel to commit liable/libel in my future writing.

1. liable, libel; 2. liable; 3. libel; 4. libel; 5. liable; 6. liable; 7. liable, libel; 8. libel; 9. libels, liable, libel; 10. liable, libel.

Mantel-Mantle

Most people pronounce these two nouns the same way (MAN-t'l), but they're spelled differently, and defined differently.

In fact, the term *mantle* has several different meanings. In what's probably its most-common use, it names a piece of outerwear, a loose cape or cloak without sleeves. It's easy to see how this literal meaning leads to one of its figurative uses—anything that covers, conceals, envelops: the mantle of night, of mist, of darkness. Or, on the favorable side, the mantle of greatness, of fame, of celebrity.

The term also refers to that part of the earth (about 1800 miles thick) between the outer crust and the core—so the earth's mantle is the part covering, or cloaking, the core.

A *mantel* is a shelf above a fireplace (sometimes the term is used to include a frame around the opening, as well as the shelf itself). To remember the difference in spelling, think of an elevated railway —or EL.

It's not hard to mentally link the horizontal railway to a horizontal beam or shelf above a fireplace. Or if you're a Civil-War buff, you can imagine the cloaked figure of Robert E. Lee, and link his last name to the -LE ending of *mantle*.

Exercise: Mantel-Mantle

1. Scientists say that there's an extremely hot core beneath the earth's mantel/mantle.

2. An outcropping of rock formed a mantel/mantle over the cave opening.

3. The bishop threw his mantel/mantle over his shoulders before going out into the rain.

4. He had little official authority, but used the mantel/mantle of his boss's position as protection.

5. Under the mantel/mantle of darkness, the thieves broke in and stole the rare vase that had been sitting on the mantel/mantle.

6. His stiff, protruding mustache formed a mantel/mantle above his thin mouth.

7. Villains were often portrayed as wearing black hats and dark, silk mantels/mantles.

8. Some celebrities think their mantels/mantles of fame give them the right to break the law.

9. After expanding his vocabulary, he found that the mantel/mantle of scholarly recognition fell around his shoulders.

10. At the student honors assembly, he was given a scholastic-achievement trophy to put on his mantel/mantle.

Pallet-Palette-Palate

When you see a forklift moving merchandise around in one of those big-box home-maintenance stores, the goods are usually sitting on a flat, portable wooden platform—a *pallet* (sometimes called a skid). The forklift projections are inserted in spaces between boards, thus protecting the merchandise.

Another fairly common meaning of pallet is "a small or makeshift bed," as a straw-filled sack (e.g., "Make me a pallet on your floor").

A *palette*, on the other hand (or other thumb) is a thin, curved board with a thumb-hole, used by artists for holding their mixed paints. By extension, it also means the range of colors used by a particular artist, or the range of colors available on a computer-graphics card.

And then there's *palate*—the roof of the mouth (the hard palate is in front; the soft palate—or velum—is in back). The term is sometimes used to mean "sense of taste," as in "Where wines are concerned, she has a discriminating palate." One memory hook is to imagine a friend who was choosy about food—you could say "My PAL ATE only the best."

All three words are commonly pronounced the same—roughly rhyming with *mallet*.

Exercise: Pallet-Palette-Palate

1. The artist squeezed paints of different colors onto her palate/pallet/palette.

2. An oral surgeon sees numerous palates/pallets/palettes.

3. Lots of lumber is used in making palates/pallets/palettes for moving merchandise.

4. My new computer-graphics program has an extensive palate/pallet/palette of colors to choose from.

5. The chicken farmer loaded crates of pullets onto palates/pallets/palettes.

6. She has a sensitive palate/pallet/palette, preferring only the best food.

7. It's the same with her sense of color; she tries to make sure the paints on her palate/pallet/palette include a variety of colors to satisfy the palate/pallet/palette of anyone who might buy her art.

8. The workers brought palates/pallets/palettes of canned goods into the store for restocking the shelves.

9. We used old wooden palates/pallets/palettes from the warehouse for a bonfire.

10. I burned my palate/pallet/palette on a toasted marshmallow.

1. palette; 2. palates; 3. pallets; 4. palette; 5. pallets; 6. palate; 7. palette, palate; 8. pallets; 9. pallets; 10. palate.

Peak-Peek-Pique

A major newspaper interchanged two of these words (using *peek* instead of *peak*) in its lead editorial—not once, but twice. So again, we see how even the best writers need to take special care with such confusables (not to mention the editors and proofreaders who let the slips of the pen slip through).

The three words *peak*, *peek*, and *pique* are pronounced pretty much the same, but they have completely different meanings.

As a noun, a *peak* is the top of something (often a mountain). As a verb, to *peak* means to reach the highest level, as in "She's still a young golfer, and her game hasn't peaked yet," or "I'm afraid he peaked too soon."

Peek can also be used as either a noun or a verb. To *peek* means to take a quick (often sneaky or surreptitious) look—"The children peeked through their interlaced fingers during the scary movie." A *peek* is the look or glance itself (as in "Take a peek at this").

Those double "e's" in *peek* give us a good memory hook, because all we have to do is think of a pair of peeking EyEs.

As a verb, *pique* means to arouse a feeling or emotion. The feeling may be pleasant ("The vocabulary quizzes piqued the students' interest") or unpleasant ("He was greatly piqued when his editorial suggestions were rudely rejected").

As a noun, *pique* refers to a feeling of irritation or resentment. "They were in a fit of pique after losing the game in the final seconds."

Note that there's a similar word (piqué, pronounced pee-KAY) that refers to a kind of cloth or fabric, or to a ballet step.

Got them straight? Maybe you should take a peek-peak-pique at the quiz to make sure.

Exercise: Peak-Peek-Pique

1. Some experts believe that the world's oil output has already peaked/peeked/piqued.

2. The strange writing on the tablets peaked/peeked/piqued the explorer's interest.

3. Would you please take a quick peak/peek/pique at this draft to see if it looks okay?

4. Her peak/peek/pique at losing the nomination was understandable, and she quickly got over it.

5. They climbed to the peak/peek/pique to take a peak/peek/pique at whatever was making the weird sounds that had peaked/peeked/piqued their interest.

6. The enticing smells from the kitchen peaked/peeked/piqued his curiosity—as well as his appetite.

7. She showed great promise as a young violinist, but some say she peaked/peeked/piqued too soon.

8. The wizard's peaked/peeked/piqued hat peaked/peeked/piqued Dorothy's interest.

9. Gollum loved puzzles, so his curiosity was peaked/peeked/piqued by the riddle about what was in the Hobbit's pockets.

10. But he flew into a fit of peak/peek/pique when he found that his ring was missing.

1. peaked; 2. piqued; 3. peek; 4. pique; 5. peak, peek, piqued; 6. piqued; 7. peaked; 8. peaked, piqued; 9. piqued; 10. pique.

Petal-Pedal-Peddle

Most people pronounce these triplets much the same way—although you will hear some variations among speakers of different dialects and subdialects. One difference is the d-t marker—some groups make a clear distinction, while others don't. For example the middle "t" in dentist may come through loud and clear, or the word may be pronounced so that it sounds a lot like *Dennis*. Neither is wrong; they're just different (although people in each group may think their way is the right way).

Back to our trio. Regardless of how they're pronounced, they are spelled differently, and have distinctly different meanings.

A *petal* is a part of a flower—as in the words from the song: "Take the petals from a rose..." And if you use a daisy for the old "Loves, me, loves me not" game, you're plucking *petals* from the flower. (The word comes from Greek *petalon*, meaning "leaf or thin plate.")

A *pedal* is the thing you put your foot on—as a bicycle pedal, or the brake pedal of a car. As a verb, *pedal* means to use pedals—most commonly, to go somewhere on your bicycle. As an adjective, the word means "of the foot," as in "The foot is the pedal extremity; toes are pedal digits." (The origin is Latin *ped*, foot.)

And to *peddle* is to offer things for sale, especially by going house to house, or by approaching customers in an outdoor setting. Of course, one who does this is a peddler.

Exercise: Petal-Pedal-Peddle

1. The girl would pedal/petal/peddle her bicycle to the village every morning.

2. She tried to pedal/petal/peddle her flowers in the market, but too many of the pedals/petals/peddles were missing.

3. The organist worked the pedals/petals/peddles rapidly with his feet.

4. The itinerant preacher pedaled/petaled/peddled his bike from house to house, pedaling/petaling/peddling his religious tracts and his ideas.

5. The corolla of the flower is made up of many pedals/petals/peddles radiating out from the center.

6. They rented a paddle-boat and pedaled/petaled/peddled around the tidal basin.

7. As a boy, he pedaled/petaled/peddled his bike around town, pedaling/petaling/peddling the local papers.

8. The kids referred to the accelerator as the "go-pedal/petal/peddle."

9. Liza, the flower girl, pedaled/petaled/peddled her pedals/petals/peddles at the train station.

10. We've probably given you enough information; it's time to press the brake pedal/petal/peddle.

1. pedal; 2. peddle, petals; 3. pedals; 4. pedaled, peddling; 5. petals; 6. pedaled; 7. pedaled, peddling; 8. pedal; 9. peddled, petals; 10. pedal.

57

Pore-Pour

Although these words probably cause fewer problems than some of the others in this book, they're interchanged often enough to deserve a little explanation.

To begin by stating the obvious, these tricky twins have the same pronunciation, but different spellings—and entirely different meanings. So let's define our terms.

To *pour* means to cause something (usually a liquid, but it could be anything in movable particles) to flow downward, often from one container to another—pouring wine from a bottle into a glass, pouring cereal into a bowl, salt into a shaker. The word's also used figuratively—to pour one's heart out, to pour criticism on someone.

To *pore* means to read or study carefully, with concentrated attention. "He was up well after midnight, poring over the strange manuscript."

Most of the nonstandard uses we've seen involve the use of *pour* when *pore* would be more acceptable: "They poured over the coded message, trying to make sense of it." You could imagine an example when either might make sense—"dozens of geology students poured/pored over the stone-studded slope." But that's quite a stretch, so this is basically a spelling problem.

As a noun, a pore is a tiny hole permitting liquid or gas to pass through—such as a pore in skin, or in the surface of a leaf.

To keep the spellings separate, you might think "pour out," and connect the "ou" vowel combination in the two words. Or you could think poRE-REad and link the RE ending of pore to the RE beginning of read. Use one of these, or make up your own—whatever works for you.

After you've pored over that explanation, you're ready to pour all your mental energy into this exercise.

Exercise: Pore-Pour

1. We sat by the river poring/pouring over the manuscript, as the water pored/poured over the falls.

2. The gravel pored/poured from the truck bed onto the road bed.

3. The students poured/pored strong coffee into their cups as they poured/pored over their notes for the upcoming exam.

4. The professor realized how long and carefully the students had pored/poured over their drafts, so he pored/poured praise on their work.

5. For hours, she poured/pored over the drawings on the cave walls.

6. She decided that the artists had sometimes ground charcoal into fine powder, pored/poured it into hollow tubes, and blown it onto the walls.

7. Some of the drawings were so beautiful that the creators must have pored/poured their hearts into their work.

8. The librarian warned us to be careful with the books, telling us that it was okay to pore/pour over them, but not to pour/pore coffee over them.

9. Dejected, he sat in the poring/pouring rain, poring/pouring over the sad state of his life.

10. Some dedicated students pore/pour all their mental energy into their studies, poring/pouring over their books until all hours.

1. poring, poured; 2. poured; 3. poured, pored; 4. pored, poured; 5. pored;
6. poured; 7. poured; 8. pore, pour; 9. pouring, poring; 10. pour, poring.

59

Cumulative Exercise:
Liable-Libel, Mantel-Mantle,
Palate-Palette-Pallet

1. An artist with too few colors on her palate/palette/pallet is liable/libel to have trouble painting complex scenes.

2. As the mantel/mantle of dusk fell, he kneeled beneath the mantel/mantle and stoked up the fire.

3. You're not as liable/libel to damage the merchandise if you pack it on palates/palettes/pallets.

4. Written slander is called liable/libel.

5. She has a discriminating palate/palette/pallet for fine wines.

6. After her cookbook became a best-seller, the mantel/mantle of fame descended on her.

7. When a reviewer accused her of plagiarism, she sued for liable/libel.

8. Gulping too quickly, he burned his palate/palette/pallet on the scalding coffee.

9. Your computer-graphics software has a widely varied palate/palette/pallet of colors.

10. If you set the vase too close to the edge of the mantel/mantle, it's liable/libel to fall off.

1. palette, liable; 2. mantle, mantel; 3. liable, pallets; 4. libel; 5. palate;
6. mantle; 7. libel; 8. palate; 9. palette; 10. mantel, liable.

Cumulative Exercise:
Peak-Peek-Pique, Pedal-Peddle-Petal,
Pore-Pour

1. After struggling to reach the peak/peek, he fell into a fit of peak/peek/pique when he caught a peak/peek/pique at the sign saying another climber had already been there.

2. Poring/pouring over the botany book, she found a picture of a flower with pedals/peddles/petals of just the color she wanted.

3. The flower-girl pored/poured water into her canteen, loaded her bouquets into the basket of her bike, then pedaled/peddled/petaled around town, pedaling/peddling/petaling her wares.

4. A young man, his interest peaked/peeked/piqued as much by the girl's smile as by her blossoms, poured/pored over the bouquets for several minutes before choosing one.

5. He began plucking pedals/peddles/petals from a daisy, peaking/peeking/piquing up at her as he said "…loves me, loves me not…"

6. The tennis player flew into a fit of peak/peek/pique when the sportswriter said she may have peaked/peeked/piqued too soon.

7. You'll have to drive fast to reach the peak/peek/pique before the mantle of darkness falls, so put the pedal/peddle/petal to the metal, and pore/pour on the petrol.

1. peak, pique, peek; 2. poring, petals; 3. poured, pedaled, peddling; 4. piqued, pored; 5. petals; 6. pique, peaking, peaked; 7. peak, pedal, pour.

Rain-Reign-Rein

We thought it might have been a typo, a simple slip of the fingertip, when we read that a new director had taken the *reigns* of leadership.

But the word was used—or misused—the same way in the next paragraph of the editorial. So we had to assume that the writer just didn't know the difference between *reigns* and *reins*.

Reins are the thin leather straps riders use to control horses—"The jockey took a firm grip on the reins." So it's an easy step from that literal usage to the figurative one of control or leadership—"She seemed eager to grasp the reins of power that came with the position."

And that sense of control associated with the word *reins* can lead to some confusion with the word *reigns*, which also connotes control or authority.

As a verb, *reign* means to rule, to govern, to wield authority and power—"The king reigned over all he surveyed." (Here's a memory hook: associate the *g* in king with the *g* in reign.) As a noun, *reign* means the time or tenure of the reigning person—"His reign lasted for eight years."

And of course there's *rain*, as in April showers, but that one seems to cause very little trouble. So now that you know the difference, grab the reins, and don't let doubts rain on your parade.

Exercise: Rain-Reign-Rein

1. Tiger grasped the rains/reigns/reins of leadership in his first golf tournaments, and has rained/reigned/rained as the favorite ever since.

2. His rain/reign/rein has endured through storms, rain/reign/rein, and fair weather.

3. The Viking leader's rain/reign/rein was short, for he was injured during a raid.

4. The pony's rains/reigns/reins were short, so the rider had to lean forward.

5. The king passed the rains/reigns/reins of control to the prince, wishing him a long and happy rain/reign/rein.

6. We may never know what ended the rain/reign/rein of the huge dinosaurs.

7. Some scientists think a huge meteorite caused darkness and rain/reign/rein that covered and cooled the earth.

8. Some Shakespearean tragedies involve plots against the raining/reigning/reining king and attempts by plotters to seize the rains/reigns/reins of power.

9. Aspiring managers must be willing, but not overly eager, to take the rains/reigns/reins of authority.

10. The movie cowboys not only held the rains/reigns/reins of their horses, but they also rained/reigned/reined supreme as movie-hero favorites for decades.

1. reins, reigned; 2. reign, rain; 3. reign; 4. reins; 5. reins, reign; 6. reign; 7. rain; 8. reigning, reins; 9. reins; 10. reins, reigned.

63

Ravage-Ravish

If you find these two words confusing, you have good reason. They look and sound a lot alike, they come from the same root word (Middle French *ravir*, from Latin *rapere*), and they overlap in meaning. But they are distinct terms, with distinct meanings.

Ravage, as it's most commonly used, means to destroy or damage greatly, to plunder. The damage can be literal and physical ("The plundering hordes swept across the valley, ravaging every village in their path"), or not ("The whole sordid affair ravaged three reputations and set the economic recovery back considerably").

Ravish has three fairly common meanings—two negative, one usually positive. Here are the bad-news meanings: 1) to seize and carry away ("The bears ravished our supplies while we were out hiking"), and 2) to rape. Notice that the negative meanings are a bit similar to the meanings of *ravage*—that's where part of the confusion comes from.

Here's a memory aid: To *ravage* is to heavily *damage*. (Notice the double a's in each word.) To *ravish* (with an *i*) means to seize, or steal, and carry off. *Lift* (also with an *i*) is a slang term meaning to steal, to carry off. So you could say "The vandals ravaged our shed and ravished the tools we had stored there."

The third meaning of *ravish* is to enchant, to overcome with emotion ("Ruby mesmerized the truckers who came into her diner; her beauty simply ravished her admirers"). This is the usual meaning of the word when it's used in lurid, bodice-ripping stories.

NOTE: The word *savage*, when used as a verb, has essentially the same meaning as *ravage*. "The critics savaged her second novel." "The rancher released a donkey into the pasture to keep the young calves from being savaged by coyotes."

Exercise: Ravage-Ravish

1. She was a ravishing/ravaging beauty.

2. The marauding raccoons ravished/ravaged our food locker during the night, and ravished/ravaged our food supplies.

3. The hungry hikers were lured by the ravishing/ravaging smell of the grilling meat.

4. The pirates swept through the coastal village, ravishing/ravaging the natives' shacks and ravishing/ravaging everything of value.

5. His image as a loyal public servant was ravished/ravaged by his attempt to sell the vacant legislative seat.

6. The ravishing/ravaging femme fatale was the sex symbol for the movie industry, and the fantasy of every pubescent male.

7. The congressman's midnight dip in the reflecting pool with the ravishing/ravaging exotic dancer made headlines.

8. The resulting publicity ravished/ravaged his reputation, while improving hers.

9. The great beauty of the goddess Venus completely ravished/ravaged all who beheld her.

10. She was a ravishing/ravaging beauty, but her low score on the vocabulary quiz ravished/ravaged her reputation as an intellectual standout.

1. ravishing; 2. ravaged, ravished; 3. ravishing; 4. ravaging, ravishing; 5. ravaged; 6. ravishing; 7. ravishing; 8. ravaged; 9. ravished; 10. ravishing, ravaged.

65

Relegate-Delegate

The underlying problem with this pair is not just that they look and sound a lot alike, but also that they sort of straddle two common meanings. One of these meanings is to send or consign to an inferior position, place, or condition; the other is to assign or refer something to be done.

It's far more common in well-edited publications to use *relegate* for the first sense: "After his disastrous performance during the aftermath of the hurricane, he was relegated to a boring, lower-level job in the boonies." "We have too many canning jars, so let's relegate some of them to the recycling bin."

And when you simply want to say "to assign (a task, etc.)," you'd most always use *delegate*: "Many new managers try to do too many things themselves, rather than judiciously delegating tasks to others."

But be careful—some good dictionaries give this last sense as one meaning of *relegate*, as in "He tends to relegate the unpleasant jobs to people he doesn't like." So although most careful writers would use *delegate* there, it's clear that not all follow that principle.

SUMMING UP: If you'd like a couple of simple rules to follow, based on what we find as the predominant practices in well edited prose, here you are.

- Use *delegate* when you mean to give or assign (a task, power, authority) to someone else.
- Use *relegate* to mean to assign to an inferior place or position, to banish.

Careful writers rarely if ever use *delegate* to mean pack off to a less-important job or position; people are much more likely to use *relegate* when *delegate* would work better. So the splash-over is largely a one-way matter.

Exercise: Relegate-Delegate

1. As a new supervisor, Ted was reluctant to delegate/relegate work to others.

2. He soon found himself delegated/relegated to a less-prestigious job.

3. Her computer was obsolete, so she delegated/relegated it to the spare-parts bin.

4. She had delegated/relegated the task of disassembling such equipment to "Ned the Nerd" Gates.

5. The indicted congressman was stripped of his powerful position and delegated/relegated to a minor subcommittee.

6. Many of us get tired of fashionable words and delegate/relegate them to the "don't use" category.

7. Gretchen delegated/relegated the task of reviewing the style manual to Argu, the editor.

8. He found that several of the so-called inviolate rules were invalid, and recommended that they be delegated/relegated to the "don't have to follow" appendix.

9. A wise parent will delegate/relegate some of the scheduled household chores to the children, and will delegate/relegate some of the less-important tasks to the "maybe we'll get around to it sometime" list.

10. It's a basic rule of good management that you can delegate/relegate some of your work, but not responsibility for ensuring that it's done.

1. delegate; 2. relegated; 3. relegated; 4. delegated; 5. relegated; 6. relegate; 7. delegated; 8. relegated; 9. delegate, relegate; 10. delegate.

67

Root-Route-Rout

First, the pronunciation. *Root* rhymes with boot; *rout* rhymes with out; and *route* can be pronounced like either of the other two.

Now for the meanings.

A *route* is a road, path, or course, as in "Let's find out what the shortest route is." It can also mean the usual course or routine, as in "The mail-carrier follows his daily route." As a verb, it means to send or direct in a certain way, or on a certain course: "Let's route this draft to Chris for comment."

To *rout* is to defeat decisively, to send fleeing: "We have met the enemy, and thoroughly routed them." As a noun, it means the defeat itself: "Well, you can only describe what my Red Sox did to your Pale Hose as another total rout."

A *root* can be the underground part of the plant that anchors it and provides nutrients. It can also be the source or origin of something, as in: "The love of money is the root of all evil." It has other, specialized meanings, as in math (e.g., the square root), and "to dig out or uncover something." And as a slang or informal term, *to root for* means "to cheer for, to support."

Exercise: Root-Route-Rout

1. A straight line has been said to be the shortest root/rout/route between two points.

2. I had hoped to give my tennis opponent a decent game, but it turned into an embarrassing root/rout/route.

3. He finally reached his destination, but only after following a circuitous root/rout/route.

4. The root/rout/route of his problem was a tendency to forget to come to class.

5. The travel agent rooted/routed us along a scenic root/rout/route.

6. We ate truffles, which had been rooted/routed out by pigs.

7. If we're going to hike that steep root/rout/route, we'd better root/rout/route around for our heavy boots.

8. If you follow this root/rout/route, you'll arrive at your goal on time.

9. The team she rooted/routed for didn't just defeat the opponents—it absolutely rooted/routed them.

10. It was a complete root/rout/route, a real trouncing.

1. route; 2. rout; 3. route; 4. root; 5. routed, route; 6. rooted; 7. route, root; 8. route; 9. rooted, routed; 10. rout.

Site-Cite-Sight

First, the easiest one. For the great majority of us, that's *sight*. Its most-common meaning as a verb is "to see." As a noun it has several meanings, including a spectacle, something worth seeing ("The view from Hanging Rock was quite a sight"), one's vision ("She has very good sight"), or something surprising or distressing ("They looked a sight after struggling through the underbrush").

Probably next-most common is *site*, which can also be used as a verb or a noun. Its most-frequent sense as a noun is position or location—"The knoll will be the site of our cabin." A similar but slightly different meaning is the exact plot of ground where something is, was, or will be located. "The site of the planned clinic was clearly marked on the application for a building permit." "Those ruins mark the site of the ancient city." As a verb, *site* means to put into place. "He ordered the men to site the artillery for maximum effect."

That leaves *cite*, which is troublesome not only because it's sometimes used when *site* would be better, but also because it has several different meanings, two them almost opposite. Its most-common use as a verb is to quote, or refer to, a passage as an authority. "She cited the ordinance on animal control in her defense." "He cited the Constitution to support his claim." In this sense, *cite* is a shortened form of *citation*, which is used in more-formal contexts. "My advisor said that my thesis needed more citations of source material."

Now for those near-opposite meanings of *cite* (or *citation*). You may be *cited* (or given a citation) for something outstandingly good you've done. "The pilot was given a citation after landing the plane safely." On the other hand, it may mean to give an official summons for an offense. "The patrolman gave her a citation for speeding." "The neighborhood association cited him for planting tomatoes in his front yard."

Exercise: Site-Cite-Sight

1. After sighting/siting/citing the speeding car, the patrolman sighted/sited/cited the driver for exceeding the speed limit.

2. It was the motorist's third sightation/sitation/citation that month.

3. In her term paper, she sighted/sited/cited the study on glaucoma, which can severely damage one's sight/site/cite.

4. That lakeside sight/site/cite looks so peaceful—let's sight/site/cite our camp there.

5. The searchers finally sighted/sited/cited the family who had been lost in the woods.

6. The bedraggled children looked a sight/site/cite, but appeared healthy.

7. The rescuers were sighted/sited/cited by the governor.

8. The view from the cabin sight/site/cite was a sight/site/cite to behold.

9. When she first sighted/sited/cited the lush valley, she knew it was the ideal sight/site/cite to build her painting studio.

10. The soldier was sighted/sited/cited for bravery after he sighted/sited/cited the enemy convoy and sighted/sited/cited his telescope in a position to observe their movements.

1. sighting, cited; 2. citation; 3. cited, sight; 4. site, site; 5. sighted; 6. sight; 7. cited; 8. site, site; 9. sighted, site; 10. cited, sighted, sited.

Stent-Stint

Most of us know *stent* as the name of a tubular structure used in medicine and surgery, such as the little mesh cylinders inserted into blood vessels to keep them open. Even though this may be the most-common use of the term, it's not the first in the history of this interesting word.

Although at least one reference we checked listed the origin of *stent* as "uncertain," most give credit to Charles Thomas Stent, a British dentist. In the mid-19th century, Dr. Stent developed a compound for making dental impressions (trademarked "Stents," possibly because his sons, also dentists, were involved).

Some years later, a Dutch plastic surgeon discovered that Stent's compound worked well as material for making molds to hold skin grafts in place. The surgeon published a paper in 1917, referring to the devices as "stents molds." Over the next several decades, other physicians gradually found more uses for the devices (including cardiovascular and urological supports), and now the term and the devices are well established.

The near-identical twin, *stint*, is not so straightforward. It has several uses, as both verb and noun. As a verb, it means to be frugal, to watch your pennies, to conserve: "We had to really stint to make our supplies last," or "We stinted almost all the time we were in college," or "The hostess sure didn't stint on the food."

As a noun, *stint* usually means a period of time, especially time spent doing something: "She did a four-year stint in the Marine Corps," or "He did his daily stint on the exercise machines." It can also mean a limit, a ration, as in "When the needy came for help, we gave without stint."

Exercise: Stent-Stint

1. While doing his stent/stint in the kitchen, Uncle Ben was not one to stent/stint on the servings.

2. Many heart-surgery patients credit their survival to the development of the stent/stint.

3. During his stent/stint as resident, he learned how surgeons implanted stents/stints.

4. We have plenty of gazpacho, so don't stent/stint when dishing it out.

5. Many tubular structures in the body can be supported or replaced by stents/stints.

6. As the economy worsens, millions of people are having to stent/stint on little luxuries.

7. The doctors and nurses worked without stent/stint as they installed stents/stints in the patients.

8. The pre-med students studied without stent/stint, often late into the night.

9. One thing they learned was how stents/stints are inserted.

10. You've worked without stent/stint on this exercise; I hope you won't need a stent/stint in your overtaxed brain.

1. stint, stint; 2. stent; 3. stint, stents; 4. stint; 5. stents; 6. stint; 7. stint, stents; 8. stint; 9. stents; 10. stint, stent.

Cumulative Exercise:
Rain-Reign-Rein, Ravage-Ravish,
Relegate-Delegate

1. The reigning/raining/reining beauty queen was a ravaging/ravishing redhead.

2. After winning the contest, she delegated/relegated her old clothes to the Goodwill box.

3. Her rivals, trying to reign/rein/rain in the expansion of her popularity, decided to ravish/ravage her reputation.

4. After taking the rains/reigns/reins of power, the president delegated/relegated several important tasks to key members of his team.

5. During his reign/rein/rain, he had to delegate/relegate some less-urgent needs to the "do-later" file.

6. He knew that some of the "loyal opposition" would try to ravage/ravish his programs.

7. Taking a firm grip on the reigns/reins/rains of leadership, he did not delegate/relegate the most-urgent tasks, but did them himself.

8. He was determined to reign/rein/rain wisely and fairly during his entire reign/rein/rain.

9. His chief of staff kept a tight reign/rein/rain on the selection process, making sure that no woman was chosen simply because she was a ravaging/ravishing beauty.

10. The police chief has been trying to think of a way to reign/rein/rain in the gangs that had been ravaging/ravishing the area.

1. reigning, ravishing; 2. relegated; 3. rein, ravage;
4. reins, delegated; 5. reign, relegate; 6. ravage; 7. reins, delegate;
8. reign, reign; 9. rein, ravishing; 10. rein, ravaging.

Cumulative Exercise:
Rout-Route-Root, Site-Sight-Cite, Stent-Stint

1. The campaign team carefully planned the rout/route/root to the White House, and didn't stent/stint on effort or funding.

2. She had her site/sight/cite clearly focused on their goal.

3. The result was a clear victory, although not quite a rout/route/root.

4. He was pleased when his commanding officer sited/sighted/cited him for a job well done, but not when the police officer sited/sighted/cited him driving too fast, and then sited/sighted/cited him for speeding.

5. The field will be the site/sight/cite of the new hospital, if the sponsoring organization doesn't stent/stint too much on funding.

6. During his overnight stent/stint in the emergency room, the surgeon implanted stents/stints in two patients.

7. As soon as the apiarist sited/cited/sighted the little knoll in the middle of the orchard, he knew it was the ideal site/sight/cite for his bee hives.

8. By choosing an unexpected root/route/rout through rough terrain, the brigade surprised the enemy, and the ensuing battle turned into an utter route/rout/root.

9. The strategic planners were cited/sited/sighted for their unstenting/unstinting dedication to duty.

1. route, stint; 2. sight; 3. rout; 4. cited, sighted, cited; 5. site, stint; 6. stint, stents; 7. sighted, site; 8. route, rout; 9. cited, unstinting.

75

Bonus Words—
A Little Lagniappe*
Rack-Wrack

You can *rack* billiard balls, or *rack* up a good score when playing. But do you *wrack* your brain, or *rack* it?

When you're talking, there's no problem, because the words are pronounced the same. But if you're writing, which do you use? The question comes up just often enough so that we feel we should know the answer, but not often enough to keep it firmly in our minds. And the answer—as well as the reasoning behind it—isn't perfectly clear, either.

Here's the short answer—"rack your brain" is standard. In this sense, rack means "to strain in mental effort."

Why do we confuse the two? One obvious reason is that they sound the same, and look a lot alike. Further, in some senses they have similar meanings. *Wrack* can mean damage, destruction, or disaster, as the wrack and ruin of the battle. And as a verb, *wrack* can mean to ruin or wreck—as in "if that boy keeps driving so fast and recklessly, he's going to wrack up the car for sure." So it's understandable that they'd sometimes be interchanged. And *rack* can mean "to torture on the rack," or by extension, to torture or torment in any way.

So it's at least a bit complicated. But as far as usage is concerned, you're safe if you write "rack your brain." Now that you know that, try not to wrack your brain (or to wreck it) when you do the exercise.

Lagniappe (lan-YAP), in its modern-day sense, is a little something extra thrown in free, as a gift to a customer.

Exercise: Rack-Wrack

1. I've been racking/wracking my brain about which word to use.

2. They showed pictures of the rack/wrack and ruin in the storm-ravaged city.

3. Don't rack/wrack your mental apparatus about how you're going to win the pool game.

4. It's hopeless, so just rack/wrack up the balls, and let's play.

5. The officers racked/wracked their minds, trying to come up with an effective battle plan.

6. After the battle, the rack/wrack and wreckage strewn about was terrible.

7. The wicked man racked/wracked his evil mind for a cruel way to torture his victims.

8. He came up with plans for the rack/wrack, a device for stretching people from end to end.

9. But when the people revolted and stormed the dungeon, they totally racked/wracked up the torturer.

10. Wanting to avoid racking/wracking up her high grade-point average, and hoping to rack/wrack up a high score on the exercise, she racked/wracked her brain for the best answer to each question.

Wreak Havoc-Wreck Havoc

The basic problem here is that some people say and write "wreck havoc," while many more insist that it should be "wreak havoc." So which is it, and what should you do?

The short answer: Don't use "wreck havoc." It's not standard usage. Now let's back up a bit and take a closer look at the matter.

We know that *wreck,* as a verb, means to destroy something—a car, or a plan. As a noun, it's the event—the wreck of the Hesperus—or the thing—a wreck of his former self. *Wreak* means to cause or inflict (as heavy damage, or punishment). And *havoc* means devastation, destruction, disorder, or chaos.

On first thought, you might say that "wreck havoc" means pretty much the same as "wreak havoc." But if you think again, you'll see that "wreak havoc" means to create destruction, while "wreck havoc" would mean something like "destroy destruction."

If you think this all sounds complicated, you're right. Fortunately, you don't have to remember all these details. There's a simple way to handle the question of which or what you should use. It's based on the short answer above.

Try to avoid *wreak havoc;* it's outdated, and at least a little fancified. So call it a cliché, and put it away. Does this mean you should use *wreck havoc?* No, that's even worse. If you must use either form, choose *wreak havoc.* But don't think there are only two choices; there are others, such as *work havoc* or *play havoc.* (In our opinion, "play havoc" would more likely be used for less-serious, less-tangible matters: "The noise is playing havoc with my concentration," while *wreak havoc* would be used more with more-serious, more-physical matters: "The missiles wreaked havoc on the building.")

With that advice in mind, try not to play havoc in doing the following exercise.

Exercise: Wreak Havoc-Wreck Havoc

1. The hurricane wrecked/wreaked havoc on the coastal settlement.

2. The mischievous boys played/wrecked havoc with classroom discipline.

3. The raiders wrecked/wreaked havoc on the foodstores.

4. The disgruntled employee wreaked/wrecked vengeance on the office.

5. The nagging anxiety about the upcoming quiz is wreaking/playing havoc with my sleep.

6. The rock slide crashed down the entire hillside, wreaking/playing havoc on the flimsy shacks.

7. The hecklers slightly disconcerted the speaker, wreaking/playing havoc with his attempt to appear calm and confident.

8. The collapse of the stock market destroyed them financially, wreaking/wrecking/playing havoc on their business enterprises.

9. After the cruel insult, he vowed to play/wreak/wreck vengeance on Fortunato.

10. Being faced with a choice between words you're not sure about can wreak/play havoc with your self-confidence.

1. wreaked; 2. played; 3. wreaked; 4. wreaked; 5. playing; 6. wreaking; 7. playing; 8. wreaking; 9. wreak; 10. play.

Afterword

So, you've worked your way through the entire book. Congratulations.

You now know how to use some of the trickiest terms in our language—words that are commonly used, and commonly misused—even by good writers and speakers.

We hope you now feel confident about the words, and that you enjoy using them. Still, you'll probably want to keep the book handy to look up anything you're not sure about—especially during the next two or three months.

And if you see or hear people misusing any of the words, go easy on them. If it feels safe, sure, give some gentle advice. But keep it friendly, please. One of your jobs as a careful user of words is to avoid hurting anyone's feelings.

Another Dirty Thirty
More Words Smart People Misuse